Straight Talk About
BINGE DRINKING

James Bow

Crabtree Publishing Company
www.crabtreebooks.com

Straight Talk About.

Produced for Crabtree Publishing by:
Infinch Solutions

Publishing Director: Ravi Lakhina

Author: James Bow

Project Controller: Vishal Obroi

Editors: John Perritano, Rebecca Sjonger

Proofreader: Shannon Welbourn

Art director: Dibakar Acharjee

Designer: Kabir

Project coordinator: Kelly Spence

Production coordinator: Margaret Amy Salter

Prepress technician: Margaret Amy Salter

Consultant: Jessica Alcock, Residential Counselor BA
Psychology, MA Child and Youth Studies

Photographs:
Cover: Piotr Marcinski/Shuterstock Inc.
Title page: Jose AS Reyes/Shutterstock Inc.; p.4: Artem
Furman/Shutterstock Inc.; p.6: Artem Furman/Shutterstock
Inc.; p.8: WittyBear/Shutterstock Inc.; p.9: Sebastian Kaulitzki/
Shutterstock Inc.; p.10: Stokkete/Shutterstock Inc.; p.10:
CREATISTA/Shutterstock Inc.; p.13: Gamzova Olga/
Shutterstock Inc.; p.14: oneinchpunch/Shutterstock Inc.; p.15:
paul prescott/Shutterstock Inc.; p.16: Todd Taulman/
Shutterstock Inc.; p.17: Burlingham/Shutterstock Inc.; p.18:
lola1960/Shutterstock Inc.; p.19: Dmitry Kalinovsky/
Shutterstock Inc.; p.20: Paul Schlemmer/
Shutterstock Inc.; p.21: Kamira/Shutterstock Inc.; p.22:
Monkey Business Images/Shutterstock Inc.; p.23:
threerocksimages/Shutterstock Inc.; p.24: Photobank
gallery/Shutterstock Inc.; p.25: Monkey Business
Images/Shutterstock Inc.; p.26: Radiokafka/Shutterstock Inc.;
p.29: Lars Zahner/ Shutterstock Inc.; p.30: WEExp/
Shutterstock Inc.; p.35: Kamira/Shutterstock Inc.; p.36: Alexey
Lysenko/Shutterstock Inc.; p.38: Olimpik/Shutterstock Inc.;
p.40: Kaponia Aliaksei/Shutterstock inc.; p.41: CREATISTA/
Shutterstock Inc.; p.43: Philip Lange/Shutterstock Inc.

Library and Archives Canada Cataloguing in Publication

Bow, James, 1972-, author
    Binge drinking / James Bow.

(Straight talk about...)
Includes index.
Issued in print and electronic formats.
ISBN 978-0-7787-2200-7 (bound).--ISBN 978-0-7787-2204-5 (pbk.).--
ISBN 978-1-4271-9975-1 (pdf).--ISBN 978-1-4271-9971-3 (html)

    1. Binge drinking--Juvenile literature. I. Title. II. Series:
Straight talk about...

HV5066.B68 2015   j616.86'1   C2014-908095-6
                                            C2014-908096-4

Library of Congress Cataloging-in-Publication Data

Bow, James.
  Binge drinking / James Bow.
      pages cm. -- (Straight talk about...)
  Includes index.
  ISBN 978-0-7787-2200-7 (reinforced library binding) --
ISBN 978-0-7787-2204-5 (pbk.) -- ISBN 978-1-4271-9975-1
(electronic pdf) -- ISBN 978-1-4271-9971-3 (electronic html)
  1. Binge drinking--Juvenile literature. 2. Binge drinking--
United States--Juvenile literature. 3. Drinking of alcoholic
beverages--Juvenile literature. 4. Youth--Alcohol use--Juvenile
literature. I. Title.

HV5135.B69 2015
362.292--dc23
                                            2014045074

Crabtree Publishing Company

www.crabtreebooks.com   1-800-387-7650

Printed in Canada/022015/MA20150101

Published in Canada
Crabtree Publishing
616 Welland Ave.
St. Catharines, ON
L2M 5V6

Published in the United States
Crabtree Publishing
PMB 59051
350 Fifth Avenue, 59th Floor
New York, NY 10118

Published in the United Kingdom
Crabtree Publishing
Maritime House
Basin Road North, Hove
BN41 1WR

Published in Australia
Crabtree Publishing
3 Charles Street
Coburg North
VIC, 3058

CONTENTS

Melissa kneels on the floor. Her head swims. The music pounds. People are laughing and dancing, but Melissa is in no mood to join in. Instead, she crouches over her friend Kim who is lying on the couch. Kim has passed out after an evening of heavy drinking. How can she sleep with all the noise and loud music?

Melissa's friends have told her to leave Kim alone. Let her sleep it off. They've told Melissa not to call an ambulance because that would kill the party.

Kim's breathing is slow and shallow. Her skin is cold. Melissa doesn't know how much alcohol Kim has consumed, but it's a lot. Kim won't wake up.

The phone is beside Melissa. Should she call 911 or do what her friends say and leave Kim as she is?

Then, Kim stops breathing.

Introduction
Dangerous and Deadly

Melissa needs to call 911. Kim is in serious trouble from binge drinking. She consumed a lot of alcohol in a very short time. Now she's showing symptoms of alcohol poisoning. She needs medical attention right away.

Melissa and Kim are not alone. In the United States, as many as 28 percent of high school students have admitted to binge drinking—drinking enough to become seriously drunk—at least once in the two weeks before they were surveyed.

Some kids drink because their friends drink. Others are curious. They see adults drinking. Binge drinking, however, can cause many problems. It can put someone in the hospital. It can lead to alcohol poisoning, which can kill you. It can also lead to making bad decisions, such as drunk driving.

Underage drinkers aren't always aware of the risks. Sadly, too many kids and teens find out about the dangers of drinking the hard way.

"Before Shelby died of alcohol poisoning, she wasn't this wild party girl. Shelby partied like most of us did. She was curious about drinking—curious about how much alcohol she could drink until she passed out. Shelby was full of energy; her motto was 'Dig life!' We all just wanted to have as much fun as we could—and to see how much we could get away with." Alyssa, aged 17.

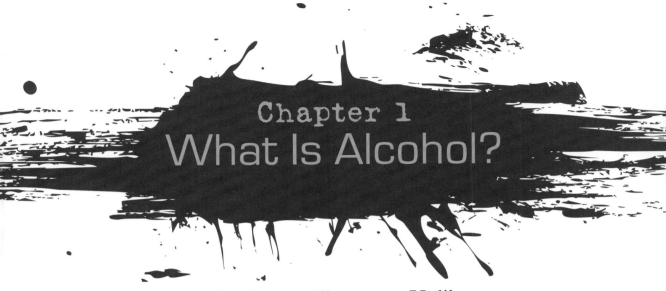

Chapter 1
What Is Alcohol?

Alcohol is a clear liquid, just like water. Unlike water, however, you can set alcohol on fire. It can also power cars, cook food, kill germs, and clean things. Alcohol is a **drug**. If you drink it, it gets into your **bloodstream** and affects your brain and your body just like any other drug would.

Alcohol comes in many forms. **Ethyl alcohol** is what humans drink. It's made when **bacteria**, such as yeast, convert the **carbohydrates**, or sugars, in plants to alcohol and heat. This process is called fermentation.

Thousands of years ago, our ancestors watched as animals ate rotting fruit and then got dizzy, and fell down, or went to sleep. Humans mimicked the animals and liked how the rotting fruit made them feel. Over time, humans figured out how to ferment fruit into alcohol. They added yeast to grapes and made wine. It was also added to wheat and barley to make beer.

Alcohol has been around almost as long as humans have been using fire. Like fire, when alcohol is used carefully, it can be useful and even helpful. Problems occur when alcohol is misused, however. Drinking too much alcohol can change the way people think and act.

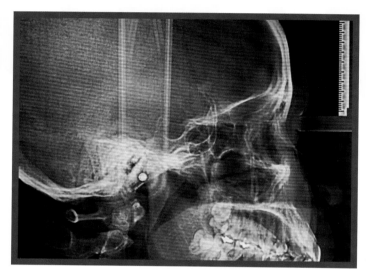

Drinking too much alcohol can impact how your brain functions.

Impact on the Brain

Ethyl alcohol is a complex **molecule** that is easily absorbed by water. This is why alcohol moves rapidly from the **digestive system** into the bloodstream. From there, alcohol travels throughout the body, affecting all organs, including the brain.

Alcohol affects a part of the brain called the *nucleus accumbens*—the brain's pleasure center. When that happens, the brain releases a natural chemical called **dopamine**. Dopamine affects how we feel. It reduces pain and makes people feel good.

Brain Cells

Alcohol's effects don't stop at releasing dopamine. Alcohol moves through the brain, getting in between **neurons** and the brain's cells. These cells send messages to one another telling our bodies what to do. Alcohol **impairs**, or weakens, the transmission of these messages.

That's why the more alcohol we drink, the more our vision is blurred. We don't hear as well as we should. Our muscles don't work the way they should and we can lose our balance.

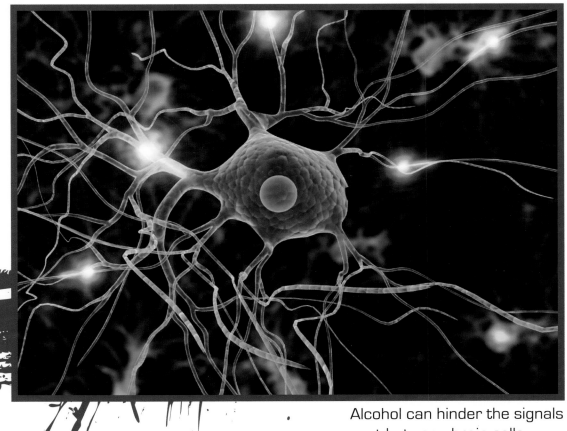

Alcohol can hinder the signals sent between brain cells.

Depression Connection

Alcohol is a **depressant**. In other words, it slows the way the brain functions. A person who consumes a lot of alcohol may feel calm, even sleepy. The elevated levels of dopamine might make us feel good, but we don't have the same control over our bodies as we do when we are **sober**.

Alcohol also alters the way we think. We become easily confused. We find it hard to concentrate and can become more emotional. Alcohol can remove **inhibitions**, which are feelings that keep us from doing things we would not normally do.

Getting Drunk

People who drink alcohol to an excess often become **intoxicated**, or drunk. Intoxicated people can hurt themselves and others. Complicated tasks such as driving a car become difficult and dangerous. Even simple tasks, such as walking a straight line, can be impossible. Alcohol can affect a person for hours, until it is filtered out of the body through sweat or urine.

The more you drink, the more time it takes for your body to rid itself of alcohol.

Peer pressure can often lead to bad decisions.

Why Do People Drink?

Kids drink for many reasons. They drink because their parents drink, or because their friends do. They see people drinking in movies and on television. Moreover, alcohol is seemingly everywhere. In many states and provinces across North America, stores have aisles stocked full of wine and beer. We see advertisements for alcoholic products in sports stadiums, magazines, on the Internet, and on billboards. It's natural to be curious about what it's like to drink.

However, most adults know the risks. Kids do not. Adults drink to be social. They drink during meals, at parties, or at other gatherings. Responsible adults never drink enough alcohol to get drunk.

What is Binge Drinking?

Binge drinking means drinking enough to raise the amount of alcohol in a person's bloodstream to 0.08 grams per deciliter of blood, or 0.08 percent. This is called the "legal limit." If the police determine that a person has more than that percentage of alcohol in his or her system while driving, they can charge that person with driving under the influence.

How many drinks does it take to get that much alcohol in your blood? It depends. Smaller people don't have to drink as much alcohol to become intoxicated as larger people. Younger people are often more affected by alcohol than older people.

By The Numbers

A study by the Centers for Disease Control and Prevention reported that 45 percent of grade 9 students admitted to binge drinking, as did 50 percent of grade 10 students, 58 percent of grade 11 students, and 62 percent of grade 12 female students.

Source: Centers for Disease Control

Why People Binge Drink

Binge drinkers want to get drunk fast. Some binge drinkers think that consuming a lot of alcohol will make them feel good. They don't realize or believe that it can just as easily make them sick, or even kill them.

Some people turn to alcohol to avoid deeper problems, such as abuse, relationship issues, or grief over a loss. Unfortunately, instead of being an escape, binge drinking usually only makes these problems worse.

Many kids binge drink because of peer pressure. Kids who don't want to drink may be afraid that others will see them as uncool, or that their friends will tease or exclude them.

Drinking too much can add to
the problems a person faces.

"I was out drinking with two friends and decided to go for a ride. We drove down the highway, but I lost control of the car, smashed into a power pole, and rolled the car over. The police arrested me and I got four years in prison for drunk driving. My friend, in the seat beside me, died. I'd trade places with him. I never intended for any of this to happen." Isaac, aged 17.

Chapter 2
Drinking and the Law

Only adults can buy or consume alcohol in Canada and the United States. In the U.S., the legal drinking age is 21. Throughout most of Canada, the legal age is 19, although in Alberta, Manitoba, and Quebec it is 18.

Stores must not sell alcohol to people under the legal drinking age. Restaurants cannot serve alcohol to those who are underage. If caught, people serving underage drinkers face stiff penalties, including fines and jail time.

Bartenders and others have to be careful whom they serve.

Drinking and selling alcoholic beverages was once banned by the U.S. Constitution.

Early Laws

In the late 19th century, many North Americans believed alcohol was dangerous for society. Too many people were getting drunk, which destroyed families and lives. As a result, people formed **temperance** movements, encouraging people not to drink alcohol.

In 1919, the United States changed its constitution and made manufacturing and drinking alcohol illegal.

That was going too far for some people. Many refused to stop drinking, and with no legal alcohol available, they turned to illegal sources. Criminals made a lot of money and became powerful by selling illegal alcohol. In 1933, the United States changed its constitution again and legalized alcohol.

Drinking and Driving

Driving under the influence of alcohol is dangerous. Alcohol slows our brains and reflexes. We're not able to make quick decisions. We can lose control of a car, causing serious accidents, injuries, and even death.

In many states and provinces, young people are not supposed to drive with any alcohol in their blood during the first stage of having their driver's license. Police officers can pull a car over if they believe the driver is under the influence of alcohol. They can administer a **breathalyzer** test, which measures how much alcohol is in the bloodstream.

Even if a drunk driver hasn't caused an accident, officers can suspend that person's driver's license immediately, or can have a drunk driver's car towed away. He or she can also face a fine and serve time in jail.

Drinking and driving can land you in hot water with the police.

Who is Responsible?

A person or business that serves alcohol to a person they know is drunk can be held responsible if that person commits a crime while under the influence. Bartenders will often ask customers to hand over their car keys if they have had too much to drink. Staff can also refuse to serve an intoxicated person. If a customer refuses to hand over his or her keys, the bartender should call the police to warn them that a drunk driver is on the road.

If you serve alcohol to people who become intoxicated, your parents might be sued if the person who drank the alcohol hurt themselves or someone else. The courts are very strict if the intoxicated person is underage.

Too drunk to drive? Give your car keys to a responsible friend or designated driver.

Driving drunk is one of the most dangerous things a person can do.

You don't have to serve alcohol to be sued. A person who was drunk at a party and got injured or hurt someone else could take the owner of the property where the party was held to court.

It's important to make sure those who are legally allowed to drink do so responsibly. If friends or family members are too drunk to drive, call them cabs or call their parents or other responsible adults to drive them home. Never serve underage guests alcohol.

By The Numbers

According to the Centers for Disease Control and Prevention, drunk driving was responsible for the deaths of 3,200 people in the United States in 2012. Thirty-one percent of all automobile accident deaths were alcohol-related. Of those deaths, 1,174 involved people under the age of 21.

Source: Centers for Disease Control

"I was just going to a party to have fun. There was alcohol there, and I tried some to see what it was like. Then I tried some more. I don't remember much after that. I only remember waking up the next morning and going home. It was only when I learned I was pregnant weeks later that I had to tell them I'd been drinking that night. I still don't remember who I had sex with." Jenna, aged 16.

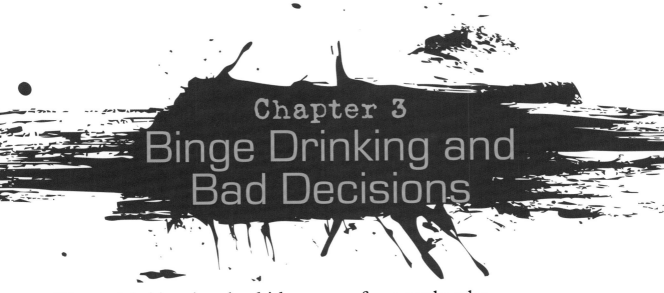

Chapter 3
Binge Drinking and Bad Decisions

Binge drinking is a bad idea, even for people who are old enough to legally drink. Alcohol is a drug that affects the brain. It slows down reflexes and it changes the way people think.

Binge drinking builds on itself. A sober person might have two drinks, not five. A drunk person, however, might continue to drink. The more alcohol a person drinks, the more his or her ability to make good decisions is impaired.

A binge drinker does not recognize his or her limit

Not Feeling Any Pain

Alcohol can make us feel good. It alters our perceptions of reality and changes our emotional responses to situations. Dopamine, released by our brains when we drink, makes us less able to feel pain. However, it also makes us more likely to hurt ourselves.

Alcohol slows our reflexes and messes with our balance. Walking becomes more difficult and we may trip over things. We might not feel any pain at the time, but we will later.

By The Numbers

In the United States, more than 100,000 people under the age of 21 visit the emergency room each year for alcohol-related injuries. People have fallen out of beds, out of windows, and off roofs while drunk.

Source: National Institute on Alcohol Abuse and Alcoholism

Some people become mean when they are drunk; others become sleepy.

22

Many people become hostile and
argumentative when they drink.

Not Thinking Straight

Alcohol dulls inhibitions. It makes people do things they
normally wouldn't do. What might seem like a stupid thing
to do while sober—such as balancing on a fence post—seems
okay to people who are drunk. That's because they are less
able to realize the consequences of their actions.

Some people become **aggressive** when they drink. They
threaten people, yell at them, or become violent. One study
suggests that alcohol plays a part in one quarter of all
assaults and 15 percent of robberies in the United States.

Alcohol can make you do things you would not normally do when it comes to having sex.

Alcohol and Sex

Drinking combined with sex can lead to a variety of problems. Sex is an emotional act to be taken seriously. When two people agree to have sex, they should be sure of their decision.

Alcohol lowers inhibitions so that people have sex when they wouldn't have done so sober. It could also lead to other bad choices, such as not using a condom to prevent pregnancy, and negative consequences, such as the transmission of **sexually transmitted diseases**. The impact of these decisions can affect people for the rest of their lives.

Some people pass out from having too much to drink, leaving them vulnerable to **sexual assault**. People sometimes slip "date-rape" drugs into drinks. Alcohol itself can be a date-rape drug, if a person uses it to make a victim **unconscious** or not aware of what they are doing.

In the United States, alcohol was a factor in 90 percent of all rapes at college campuses. Even when the sex was **consensual**, at least one in five college students failed to practice **safe sex** while drunk.

In the United Kingdom, one survey concluded that 28 percent of young adults had sex with someone they wouldn't normally have chosen, and blamed alcohol as a factor in most cases.

Some people will put date-rape drugs into alcoholic drinks.

Serious Consequences

The three leading causes of death among American teenagers are car accidents, murder, and suicides. In each of those instances, alcohol can play a role. Each year, the National Institute on Alcohol Abuse and Alcoholism linked alcohol abuse to more than 5,000 deaths of Americans under the age of 21.

According to the Harvard School of Public Health, more than one in three binge drinkers admit their schoolwork has suffered due to binge drinking. Each year, more than 690,000 American college students are assaulted by another student who has been binge drinking. Moreover, more than 97,000 American college students are victims of alcohol-related sexual assault each year.

Binge drinking is a major problem on college campuses.

The Effects of Alcohol

The following chart looks at the different effects of alcohol on the body and its impact on driving abilities.

Blood Alcohol Concentration	Number of Drinks in a 140 pound/63.5 kilogram man	Number of drinks in a 120 pound/54.4 kilogram woman	Usual Effects	Impact on Drivers
0.02%	2/3 of a drink	1/2 of a drink	• Change of mood • Some loss of judgment	• Less able to track a moving target • Less able to do two things at once
0.05%	2 drinks	4/5 of a drink	• Less alert • Impaired judgment	• Difficulty steering • Less able to respond to emergency situations
0.08% (beyond the legal limit)	3 drinks	2 drinks	• Balance problems • Slurred speech • Distorted vision and hearing	• Less able to control the speed of the car • Less able to see things
0.10%	3 2/3 drinks	2 3/4 drinks	• Much slower reaction times	• Less able to stay in the same lane or brake on time.
0.15%	5 2/3 drinks	3 1/3 drinks	• Loss of balance • Vomiting	• Severe danger of losing control of the car
0.27%	10 drinks	6 drinks	• Death is possible	

Sources: National Highway Traffic Safety Administration; National Institute on Alcohol Abuse and Alcoholism; American Medical Association; National Commission Against Drunk Driving

Myths and Facts about Binge Drinking

Myth: I don't have to worry about underage drinking in my own home. The law doesn't cover it.

Fact: Most American states and Canadian provinces have laws that can charge adults with a crime if underage kids drink alcohol in their homes. This doesn't include the legal problems that can result if binge drinking leads to kids getting hurt, property damage, or crimes being committed.

Myth: They serve some alcoholic drinks like vodka in small glasses. Doesn't that mean I'm drinking less alcohol than if I drink a bottle of beer?

Fact: No. A bottle of beer and a small glass of vodka can have the same amount of alcohol. The vodka's alcohol content is more concentrated than the alcohol in a beer.

Myth: Vomiting can help you get sober quickly.

Fact: Alcohol is absorbed into the bloodstream almost immediately. Vomiting may expel the small amount of alcohol still in your stomach, but the alcohol is already in your system.

Myth: Drinking coffee or taking a cold shower will make you sober.

Fact: Drinking coffee or a splash of cold water can make someone feel more alert, but the alcohol is still affecting the brain, slowing down reactions, and keeping a person from thinking straight. It takes an average person three hours for his or her body to get rid of the alcohol contained in two drinks. The more a person drinks, the longer it takes.

Myth: Alcohol warms up our bodies.

Fact: Alcohol makes a person feel warmer by opening up the **blood vessels** and letting the blood flow through the body. This actually makes it easier for a body to lose heat. Why should this be a concern? Because teens walking home from parties on cold winter nights after drinking heavily have died from **hypothermia**. Not only did their body temperatures drop, they were too drunk to realize they were freezing to death.

Vomiting does not help you sober up.

"One night, I woke up in the hospital, with blood all over me. I had no idea how I got there. Mom was next to me, crying. Someone had thrown a bottle and I had fallen and hit my head. It was scary and I told myself: 'Never again.' But as soon as I was discharged, I got drunk on vodka."
Maurice, aged 17.

Chapter 4
Binge Drinking and Your Health

Alcohol's effects aren't limited to the brain. It can impact the body quickly and for years to come. Alcohol is absorbed through the stomach lining and moves through the bloodstream.

As alcohol starts to affect the brain, a number of things happen. Your sense of balance will be off, and the delayed movement of your muscles makes it harder to stand. Your vision might become blurry, and sounds will become distorted. You may start feeling nauseous. If you keep drinking, you might throw up.

What's going on here? The alcohol is poisoning you. It is getting in the way of the connections in your brain and slowing your reflexes. The alcohol is confusing the messages the brain is sending to the arms and legs. This also affects the muscles that control talking and breathing. It can even impact the heart.

Alcohol Poisoning

Alcohol poisoning can be deadly. Voluntary muscle movements are not the only movements affected. Alcohol also impairs involuntary muscles, such as the ones that help your lungs to breathe and your heart to beat.

People suffering from alcohol poisoning often feel faint and may become unconscious. Their breathing slows to less than nine breaths per minute. Their lungs may even stop working for more than ten seconds at a time. Their hearts start to beat irregularly. With so much alcohol and little oxygen in the blood, their skin begins to looks pale or blue. It feels cold and clammy.

People can choke to death on their own vomit. They can fall victim to a **seizure**, meaning that their bodies will jerk about, or become rigid. They may fall into **comas**. These people could stop breathing, or their hearts could stop beating.

By The Numbers

In the United States, according to the National Institute on Alcohol Abuse and Alcoholism, more than 30,000 teenagers and college students have had to go to the hospital due to alcohol poisoning.

Source: National Institute on Alcohol Abuse and Alcoholism

Calling 911

If someone is showing any signs of alcohol poisoning after binge drinking, call 911 immediately.

As you wait for help, make sure the intoxicated person is resting on his or her side, facing slightly downward. Put pillows against the person's back to make sure he or she stays in this position. This will prevent him or her from choking on vomit. Do not leave the person until medical help arrives.

Even if the person wakes up, it is good that you called 911. It is better for him or her to be angry and alive than dead.

Long-Term Health Effects

People who routinely binge drink permanently damage their bodies. Too much alcohol in the body for too long can lead to medical problems, including high blood pressure and **stroke**. Alcohol also causes liver disease and stomach ulcers. It can even damage the brain.

Alcohol's effect on the brain is especially troublesome for kids and teens whose brains are still developing. Your brain doesn't stop developing until you turn 25. Alcohol can slow that process, which can affect you later in life. Young binge drinkers might have memory problems or mental health issues, including depression and **dementia**, as adults.

Alcohol and Addiction

For some people, binge drinking can lead to alcohol addiction. An addict's body gets so used to having drugs in its system that it starts to react badly when a drug isn't there.

Alcoholics, or people who are addicted to alcohol, experience withdrawal symptoms when they stop drinking. They feel anxious, their hands shake, they feel sick, they're tired, and they can get angry easily or become depressed. To feel better, an alcoholic will drink more, continuing the cycle.

People who regularly drink too much often find that it affects their lives and the people around them negatively. Alcoholics' work and family relationships suffer. All they want to do is drink. This can cause a lot of pain and tension between the addict and his or her friends and family.

By The Numbers

- One in four people who start drinking before the age of 17 develop an addiction to alcohol.
- One out of every 10 people who started drinking after the age of 21 develop an addiction to alcohol.

Source: National Institute on Alcohol Abuse and Alcoholism

Recovering

Recovering from alcohol addiction is not an easy task. In addition to physical withdrawal symptoms, many former addicts feel they have to watch themselves all the time so they don't slip back into their drinking habits.

Organizations such as Alcoholics Anonymous and Alateen (see page 46) offer support to alcoholics to help them stay away from alcohol. Battling alcohol addiction is an ongoing process that may never truly end.

If you think you or a friend has a drinking problem, check out the section called "Signs and Symptoms of Alcohol Addiction" in this chapter and follow the instructions.

One drink is one too many for recovering alcoholics.

The 1-2-3 Rule

If you are under the legal drinking age, you should not be drinking. Even adults have to be careful about the amount of alcohol they consume. Responsible adults stick to the 1-2-3 rule: Never drink more than 1 serving of alcohol an hour, or 2 servings in a day, or 3 servings in a week.

Alcohol and Dehydration

Alcohol can rob the body of water. That's because the kidneys work overtime to remove alcohol from the system through the passing of urine, a process that requires a lot of water. Even more water is lost when a person vomits. Sometimes the loss of water is so severe that drinkers can become **dehydrated**, which can lead to muscle cramps and seizures.

If someone is suffering from dehydration from binge drinking or vomiting, make sure he or she drinks water, or clear, uncarbonated soft drinks. The soda should not be **caffeinated**, as caffeine also dehydrates the body.

Signs and Symptoms of Alcohol Addiction

How do you know if you or someone you know has an alcohol problem? Here are some telltale signs of alcoholism:

- when you feel guilty or ashamed about your drinking, but can't stop
- when you lie to others about your drinking
- when you regularly drink more alcohol than you intended to drink
- you feel that you "need" a drink in order to relax or feel better
- when drinking interferes with your schoolwork or keeps you from doing important tasks
- when it takes much more alcohol to give you the same "buzz" or feelings you had when you first drank alcohol (this is a sign that your body is developing a tolerance)
- when not drinking alcohol makes you feel anxious, shaky, nauseous, tired, irritable, or depressed (these are withdrawal symptoms)

If you have these symptoms, get help. Talk to someone you trust or call one of the helplines listed on page 46.

If you know someone who has these symptoms, talk to that person. Let him or her know that you are worried and suggest ways to get help. Look for other people to help, too. Find a responsible adult and tell that person what is going on.

"I genuinely had not realized how much I had been drinking and I was really shocked to discover how bad it had been. I saw a substance abuse worker named Simon, and together we worked out my issues with alcohol. I'm really lucky that I have had my family and friends around to support me. I can't thank them enough." Karen, aged 19.

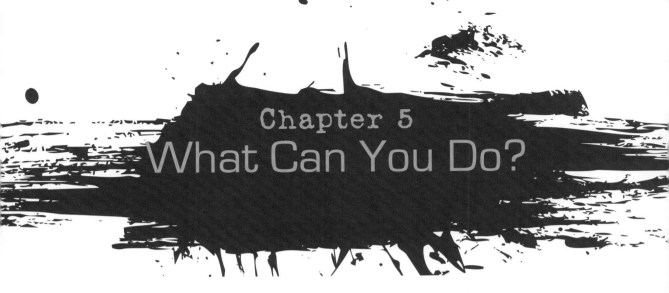

Chapter 5
What Can You Do?

A lot of binge drinking happens because people do not have the support needed to help them stop. Their parents or other adults in their lives might also binge drink. Some turn to drinking as a way to cope with their emotions and problems. Others find themselves among kids their age who are drinking and are encouraged to do the same.

If you are uncomfortable with binge drinking, that means you understand that there are risks. That's good. Now you can take the next steps you need to not binge drink.

Moreover, if you don't drink, but know a family member or friend who does, you can help them find the help they need. You can be the one who saves their life.

Good friends can help you avoid binge drinking.

Avoiding Binge Drinking

You can lessen peer pressure by surrounding yourself with people who will not push you to drink. Since a lot of binge drinking happens at parties where alcohol is present, remember to be responsible and avoid the temptation to drink.

If you're going to a party, go with friends you know will stay with you and keep you safe. They'll be there if the pressure to drink becomes too much. Sometimes it's easier to leave as a group than on your own.

You want your friends to stand by you, and so you need to also stand by your friends. Keep an eye on them and if they look like they might be getting into trouble, step in and help them get out of a bad situation.

Let Your Family Know

Parents and family members will also keep you safe. When you go to a party, tell them where you're going and what you're going to be doing. They also need to know whom you're going with and when you will be home. If you keep these promises, it will also show your parents that you are growing into a responsible adult.

Sometimes family support isn't available, especially if a parent has an alcohol problem. Talk to a reliable adult, such as a teacher, or an aunt or uncle. If that's not possible, call a helpline such as Alateen. This group helps teens deal with alcohol-related issues.

Don't be afraid to talk to an adult about any alcohol-related issues you might have.

How to Say No

A lot of binge drinking occurs because of peer pressure. It can be hard to say "no" to your friends, but if you find yourself in a situation where people are pushing you to drink, here's how you can handle it:

• Remind yourself that your body belongs to you, and you don't have to do anything you don't want to do.

• Remember that giving in to peer pressure is not going to make people magically like you.

• Ask yourself why people might be pressuring you. Maybe they're afraid of people who are different from themselves. Maybe they're making up the rules so that they fit in and you don't. Either way, they're not doing it because they like you.

If you're ever in a situation where you don't want to drink, tell your friends by saying something like, "No, thanks. I'm fine right now." Most people will accept your answer. You don't have to justify your reasons for not drinking. If they badger you, tell them, "my parents would kill me if they found out," or "that stuff makes me sick," or "I'm just not into that." If the pressure continues, just walk away. Go hang out with other friends or someone who you trust.

You Are Not Alone

Unfortunately, binge drinking is a common problem. However, many young people have found ways to deal with it. There are people you can talk to who can help you stay away from binge drinking. And if you think you have an alcohol addiction, there are people who can help you get through your problem.

The first step is admitting you have a problem. Once you do that, you can reach out to your parents, teachers, and responsible friends. There are numbers you can call if you need help right away, including 911, especially if there is a medical emergency. There are also helplines and websites run by trained professionals who know what you are going through.

As people get older and more experienced, they usually understand the risks of alcohol and are able to deal with it responsibly. By staying true to yourself and surrounding yourself with responsible people you trust, you can avoid the problems that binge drinking brings.

Don't let binge drinking get the best of you.

Hot Topics
Q&A

What does it mean when someone can "hold their liquor"?

A: Alcohol affects everybody differently. For some people, it doesn't take many drinks to feel drunk. They may not be able to drink very much before they throw up. Other people seem to be able to drink a lot without showing some of the signs of being drunk. It is said these people can "hold their liquor."

This ability does not protect them from alcohol problems. Alcohol still affects their bodies and makes them a danger behind the steering wheel. In fact, their ability to "hold their liquor" puts them at a higher risk of developing alcohol addiction, since they are able to drink more when they binge drink.

I'm taking some medicine my doctor prescribed. Should I worry about drinking alcohol?

A: Yes. Alcohol is a drug, and like all drugs, it can change the way medication works in your body. **Side effects** of mixing alcohol and medicine include being extra sleepy, changes to your heart rate and blood pressure, dizziness, stomach bleeding, and more. These side effects can be serious enough to put you in the hospital. When you pick up your medicine from a pharmacist, he or she will tell you some of the things you shouldn't be taking while you are on it. Listen to these warnings. If the **pharmacist** tells you never to drink alcohol while taking your medicine, don't do it.

Some non-prescription medicines like cough syrups, allergy pills, and even some herbal remedies do not mix well with alcohol.

The National Institute on Alcohol Abuse and Alcoholism has a web page

http://pubs.niaaa.nih.gov/publications/Medicine/medicine.htm

listing common medications and how they react with alcohol. Also, check the labels on these medicines: if they warn against drinking alcohol while taking the medicine, don't drink alcohol.

And, of course, if you are below the legal drinking age, you should not be drinking alcohol.

What's a hangover? What should I do?

A: A hangover is how the body reacts to a period of heavy drinking. The body works hard to get rid of alcohol in the bloodstream. It makes a drunken person tired. He or she will probably have a headache, and his or her stomach may feel queasy. The person's muscles are sore and his or her eyes are itchy and burning. Many people will often complain of getting the "spins," in which the room seemingly turns around and around. People will often get dry mouth because they are dehydrated. Many of these symptoms are because the body is dehydrated. Alcohol has also robbed the body of nutrients.

Some say that a good cure for a hangover is another drink. This is a very dangerous myth. The last thing the body needs is more alcohol. Instead, drink water. Fruit juices will also help put back some of the blood sugar the alcohol removed.

Other Resources

The following websites will provide you with trustworthy information about binge drinking.

TeenHealth Binge Drinking

kidshealth.org/teen/drug_alcohol/alcohol/binge_drink.html
This webpage is an online resource for teens with info on how to deal with binge drinking. It is part of a larger website dealing with a number of kids' and teen health issues.

PBS Kids–It's My Life–Thinking About Drinking

pbskids.org/itsmylife/body/alcohol/
This webpage is for kids and parents. It discusses alcohol issues in detail.

In the United States

Alateen

www.al-anon.alateen.org
1-888-425-2666
This is a national organization that works with Alcoholics Anonymous, and is set up and organized by teenagers who have suffered from alcohol problems. It offers support, counseling, group meetings, and ways to cope with alcohol addiction.

TeensHealth

teenshealth.org

This is a safe and private place online for teens who need accurate and honest information about the health issues that affect them.

The Trevor Project

www.thetrevorproject.org

1-866-4-U-TREVOR (1-866-488-7386)

If you are considering suicide or need help, call the 24-hour Trevor Project now.

In Canada

Alateen

www.al-anon.alateen.org

1-888-425-2666

As in the United States, this organization has teenagers who have dealt with their own alcohol problems helping other teens with similar issues. The toll-free number and the website offers support to Canadian teens as well as Americans, including how to find local support groups.

Kids Help Phone

www.kidshelpphone.ca

1-800-668-6868

This is a Canadian crisis helpline for boys and girls, operated 24 hours a day, 365 days a year. Calls are confidential. Trained professionals offer counseling on many subjects, including abuse, drug and alcohol issues, parenting problems, school problems, and suicide prevention.

Glossary

Note: Words appearing in boldface but not in the glossary have been explained in the text.

assault An unlawful physical attack on a person

bloodstream Your blood moving through your body

blood vessels The veins and arteries where your blood moves through your body

breathalyzer A machine that measures the amount of alcohol in the bloodstream

caffeinated A drink with caffeine in it, such as coffee, and certain types of soda

coma When your body goes deeply unconscious for a long period of time

consensual When you agree to do something

dehydrate When a lot of water has been taken out of something or someone

dementia Permanent brain damage resulting in memory loss, personality changes, and impaired reasoning

depressant A drug that slows down the processes in the brain, making a person sleepy or less alert

digestive system Your stomach and intestines, which take what you eat and drink and break it down into stuff your body uses

drug An illegal and often harmful substance that people take for pleasure

hypothermia When your body gets so cold, it starts to shut down and you freeze to death

inhibitions Feelings that make a person feel uncomfortable when doing something

intoxicated When someone has drunk enough alcohol to lose control of his or her behavior

molecule The smallest piece of a substance; a molecule is made up of two or more atoms

neurons Nerve cells

pharmacist A person who works with doctors to make sure you have the right medicine for whatever you need

safe sex Consensual sex between two people that's done with proper birth control to prevent pregnancy and the spread of sexually transmitted diseases

sexual assault Any sexual act that is forced on somebody who doesn't want it

sexually transmitted disease A disease that is spread through unprotected sex

side effects Something a drug does to the body in addition to what it is supposed to do

sober When a person's mind is unaffected by drugs or alcohol

stroke A stoppage of blood flow to the brain that causes parts of the brain to malfunction

temperance Avoiding or abstaining from alcoholic beverages

Index